'There is something delicious about writing the first words of a story. You never quite know where they'll take you.

Mine took me here. Where I belong.'

PUFFIN BOOKS is part of the Penguin Random House
group of companies whose addresses can be found
at global.penguinrandomhouse.com.

First published 2022
Text copyright and decorative illustrations
© Victoria and Albert Museum, London, 2022
Written by Katie Woolley
Illustrated by Ginnie Hsu
The moral right of the author and illustrator has been asserted
Printed in China   001
ISBN: 978-0-241-48045-8

Picture Credits

p. 6: Photograph of young Beatrix, courtesy of the Warne Archive
p. 7: Photograph of Beatrix and her brother, courtesy of the Victoria and Albert Museum and Frederick Warne & Co.; schoolroom drawing, courtesy of the Victoria and Albert Museum and Frederick Warne & Co.
p. 8 & 9: Sketches of a sleeping dormouse and beetles, courtesy of the Victoria and Albert Museum and Frederick Warne & Co.; sketches of flowers, courtesy of the Victoria and Albert Museum and Frederick Warne & Co.
p. 11: Photograph and sketches, courtesy of the Victoria and Albert Museum and Frederick Warne & Co.
p. 12: Picture letter © Frederick Warne & Co. 1993; Peter Rabbit book illustration © Frederick Warne & Co. 1902, 2002
p. 13: Image from *The Tale of Peter Rabbit* and covers, courtesy of Frederick Warne & Co.
p. 14 & 15: Book covers © Frederick Warne & Co. 1903, 1904, 1905, 2002
p. 16: Images from *The Tailor of Gloucester* © Frederick Warne & Co. 1903, 2002

p. 17: Photograph of waistcoat © Victoria and Albert Museum, London; manuscript and cover of *The Tailor of Gloucester*, courtesy of Frederick Warne & Co.
p. 19: Photograph of Peter Rabbit toy, courtesy of Frederick Warne & Co.
p. 21: Top photograph of Herdwick Sheep, courtesy of the National Trust and Frederick Warne & Co.; lower photograph of Herdwick sheep, courtesy of a private collector
p. 22: Photograph of Norman Warne, courtesy of a private collector; photograph of the Warne family, courtesy of a private collector
p. 23: Photograph of Beatrix Potter and William Heelis, courtesy of Frederick Warne & Co.
p. 27: Photograph of Beatrix Potter with Girl Guides, courtesy of the Girl Guides Association; photograph of Beatrix Potter with Kep, courtesy of the National Trust
p. 28: Photograph of Hill Top, courtesy of a private collector

Beatrix Potter

Artist · Conservationist · Pioneer

Discover the world of art and design through the V&A Introduces series. The Victoria and Albert Museum is the world's leading museum of art and design and houses over 2.3 million objects spanning over 5,000 years of human creativity. Inspired by its exhibitions, collections and heroes, this collectable series brings the wonder of the designed world to all!

Young Beatrix

Helen Beatrix Potter was born in London, England, on 28 July 1866. She grew up in a grand townhouse with her mother, father and her younger brother, Walter Bertram.

Beatrix as a child. She spent a lot of her childhood on her own.

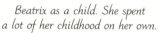

Beatrix's family lived at no. 2 Bolton Gardens in Kensington, London.

Family life

Beatrix's family was very rich. Her parents had money from the cotton trade in the north of England. Her father, Rupert Potter, was a barrister, but he spent his time pursuing an interest in art, especially photography, and chatting about politics with his friends.

His wife, Helen, was also a passionate artist. She loved to paint watercolour landscapes and was skilled at embroidery.

Beatrix was very close to her brother.

Beatrix drew this corner of her schoolroom in 1885, when she was 19 years old.

The schoolroom

Like many young children of the Victorian era, Beatrix did not see her parents very often. She was looked after by a nanny and had lessons with a governess.

Beatrix and Bertram loved animals, and would sneak them into their nursery hidden in paper bags! Their pets included mice, frogs, lizards and even a bat!

Writing and Drawing

Lost in a book

Beatrix and her brother loved to draw and sketch, just like their parents. As a little girl, Beatrix lost herself in stories and she was inspired by the illustrations. She would copy the pictures and recreate the characters.

Beatrix would also spend hours drawing pictures of her pets. When her parents saw that she had real talent, they arranged for her to be taught by an art teacher.

Beatrix did not enjoy these lessons very much because the teacher wouldn't let her paint as she wanted to. When her teacher left, Beatrix would get out her paints once more and do it her own way.

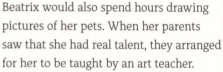

Pets and plants

Beatrix improved her drawing by studying the animals and plants around her. Her early sketchbooks are filled with flowers, rabbits and ducks. She practised and practised until she could draw each one perfectly.

By the age of nine, she was an acomplished artist. She also loved to write, and by 14 she had created her own code that she used to record the world around her in a secret journal. Beatrix was becoming a storyteller.

Escape to the Country

Life in London was often lonely for Beatrix when her brother went to school, but they had many fun-filled adventures when the family escaped the hustle and bustle of city life.

The journey north

Every year, the Potters would pack up the entire household and head off on holiday. It must have been quite a sight because servants, horses, carriages, luggage and even pets all headed north by train.

The family often went to Scotland for the summer, but in 1882 they rented Wray Castle in Windermere. The family returned to the Lake District every year until 1892, and from 1896 onwards.

The servants would leave a few days early to get everything ready.

Beatrix and Bertram loved to explore the countryside. They spent every minute outside, drawing the hills and valleys, and the wildflowers, fungi and animals they found.

Beatrix had two favourite pet rabbits that went with her everywhere, even to the Lake District. They were called Mr Benjamin Bouncer and Peter Piper. Later they became the inspiration for her famous characters: Benjamin Bunny and Peter Rabbit.

Beatrix did not give up sketching her rabbits until she was happy with them.

The Tale of Peter Rabbit

In September 1893, Beatrix wrote a story inspired by Peter Piper and sent it to a little boy who was ill. Noel was the son of Annie Moore, Beatrix's former governess. The two women had since become friends, and Beatrix often wrote to Annie and her children.

A cheeky hero

Noel and his family quickly fell in love with Peter Rabbit. Beatrix continued to send letters and stories about Peter and his friends to all the Moore children.

'My dear Noel, I don't know what to write to you, so I shall tell you a story about four little rabbits whose names are Flopsy, Mopsy, Cotton-tail and Peter.'

Eventually she decided to turn Peter's tale into a real book! Six publishers turned her down but Beatrix refused to give up.

Bright, bold and blue!

Beatrix printed 250 copies herself. She sold every last one!

Eventually Frederick Warne & Company decided to publish Peter's story, as long as Beatrix agreed to re-illustrate the book's drawings in colour.

Beatrix did so but she had some ideas of her own, too. She wanted the books to be small enough 'to fit in children's hands', and not too expensive.

In October 1902, Warne's edition of The Tale of Peter Rabbit was published. Each copy cost just one shilling.

The Lake District

Beatrix wrote twenty-three tales, with her last one, *The Tale of Little Pig Robinson*, published in 1930. All her stories were inspired by Beatrix's love of nature and the great outdoors.

In 1897, she heard of squirrels crossing Derwentwater to gather nuts on an island. These little squirrels would later inspire *The Tale of Squirrel Nutkin*.

landscapes in miniature

She sent the story of *Squirrel Nutkin* to Norah Moore, who loved the antics of the little squirrel. So, too, did her editor Norman Warne, who wanted another story after the success of *The Tale of Peter Rabbit*.

Then, while on holiday at Fawe Park in 1903, she filled a sketchbook with background detail for three tales at once: *Squirrel Nutkin, Mrs. Tiggy-Winkle* and *Benjamin Bunny*.

Beatrix continued to write at least one story a year for the next eleven years. At first, they featured friendly animal characters living amongst the beauty of the Lakes.

Sights, sketches and stories

'Two disagreeable people'

But, by 1912, Beatrix didn't want to write about 'well-behaved people' any more. Her next book told the tale of two villains, always squabbling and trying to outwit one another – the fearsome Mr. Tod and the grumpy Tommy Brock.

The TAILOR of GLOUCESTER

Beatrix often found inspiration for her tales in unlikely places. *The Tailor of Gloucester* is based on the true story of a tailor who was making a waistcoat for the town mayor.

When the light faded, John Prichard left the waistcoat on his workbench for the night. The next morning, he discovered the garment had been stitched together as he slept.

Fairies or mice?

John thought it was the work of fairies. In fact, the waistcoat was completed by two of the tailor's own apprentices. In *The Tailor of Gloucester* it is mice.

The mice in the story were based on Beatrix's pet mice. As with her rabbits, Beatrix even took her mice to the Lake District while she sketched the tale.

Museum moments

Beatrix's drawing of the waistcoat matched one that she had seen on display at the South Kensington Museum (now the V&A Museum).

In a letter to her editor, Norman, she said, *'I have been delighted to find I may draw some of the most beautiful 18th century clothes at S. Kensington museum.'*

The Tailor of Gloucester remained one of Beatrix's favourites *'amongst my little books'*.

The waistcoat is still kept at the museum.

The first 20,000 copies quickly sold out and Warne had to print an extra 6,000 to keep up with demand.

The Businesswoman

Beatrix wasn't only a master storyteller and skilled artist; she was also a pioneering businesswoman. She was determined that people should know that she was the person behind Peter Rabbit.

Side-shows

Her characters were turned into toys and games, wallpaper, playing cards, tea sets and biscuit tins that sold all around the world. Beatrix called the merchandise 'side-shows'.

The little doll

In 1903, Beatrix told Norman Warne that she was making a doll of Peter Rabbit. Beatrix registered her patent that year. This was a very unusual thing to do, especially for a woman. But it was also clever. Beatrix wanted to protect her work and her original drawings.

Her prototype even included whiskers made from hair pulled out of a brush!

Fan mail

Every year, Beatrix was sent hundreds of letters, and she always took the time to reply. Sometimes she sent back tiny letters written by the characters, and included new drawings and snippets of information about Peter and his world.

By now, the world knew about Beatrix Potter. She was famous!

Hill Top Farm

By 1905, Beatrix had enough money from her books to leave London and buy her own home. She bought Hill Top Farm in Near Sawrey in the Lake District.

The farmhouse and gardens needed work. Within a year, she had added paths and flowerbeds, and she had even bought some sheep and cows to keep on the land.

Beatrix had visited Near Sawrey with her parents as a girl. She thought it 'nearly perfect'.

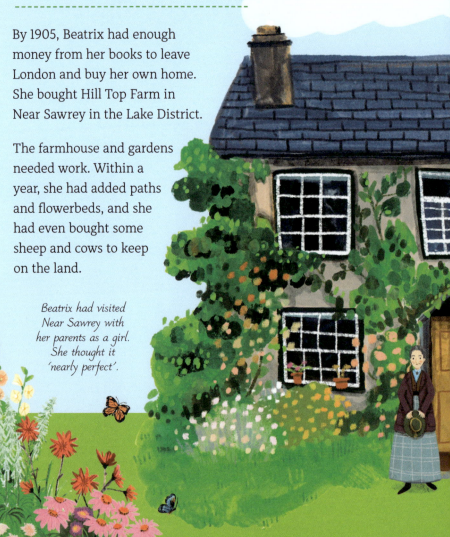

Herdwick sheep

Along with her shepherd Tom Storey, Beatrix bred and raised a large herd of over 1,000 Herdwick sheep, a special breed that have been in the Lake District for centuries. She entered the animals into shows and won lots of prizes, becoming a passionate and respected breeder of Herdwick sheep. Beatrix was even the first woman elected as president of the Herdwick Sheep Breeders' Association.

Love & Marriage

In 1905, the same year that Beatrix bought Hill Top Farm, her editor, Norman Warne, proposed to her and she accepted.

Beatrix's parents were not pleased with her engagement. Despite her parents' fortunes having come from trade, they thought Norman's job as a publisher was not good enough for their daughter.

The Warne family

A secret engagement

Beatrix wore Norman's ring, but there was no big announcement. Sadly, one month after proposing, Norman died suddenly. He was just 37 years old. Beatrix was devastated. She found comfort in her next book, *The Tale of Mrs. Tiggy-Winkle*.

Trouble in paradise

After Norman died, Beatrix chose to spend more time at Hill Top Farm. But, little by little, the landscape was changing around it. More roads and railways were being constructed, more trees were being cut down and more houses were being built on farmland. With the help of a local solicitor, William Heelis, Beatrix began to buy farms and land in the Lake District to protect the countryside for the future.

A country wife

Beatrix and William spent a lot of time together, visiting farms and talking about how to protect the Lakes. In 1912, seven years after Norman's death, William proposed to Beatrix.

Once more, her parents were unhappy, but the wedding went ahead anyway. The married couple moved into her larger farmhouse, Castle Cottage, in 1913.

The National Trust

Farm life and country living were not easy. Beatrix could often be found mending pipes, bringing in the hay, feeding the animals and fixing the roof. Just like Beatrix, her characters were kept busy too. Mrs. Tiggy-Winkle always had a mound of washing to do, and Mrs. Rabbit had goods to sell, housework to finish and a family to raise.

Protecting Peter

Even though Beatrix was now a busy farmer, she made sure she had time to protect the landscape that inspired her stories. She bought and saved land from development and worked with the co-founders of the National Trust – an organization set up in 1895 – to protect the changing countryside.

Defender of the Lakes

Beatrix first met one of the co-founders of the National Trust, when she was a teenager. The Potters were friends with the Rawnsleys. Hardwicke Rawnsley was the vicar at Wray, and he shared Beatrix's passion for the countryside.

Throughout their lives, Beatrix and Hardwicke never stopped working to protect their local landscape.

Hardwicke Rawnsley helped set up the National Trust. He was nicknamed 'Defender of the Lakes'.

Country Living

As Beatrix got older, writing and painting became hard to do as her eyesight failed. Instead, she kept busy by looking after the land, its people and its animals. She had always preferred country living to life in the town.

Her stories describe country life fondly, with the kettle always boiling for when visitors drop in, washing drying by the fire and children frolicking in the countryside and getting up to mischief.

Beatrix wanted everyone to find joy at the Lakes. Every year, she welcomed lots of visitors from all around the world.

Care and compassion

But country life was also hard. When Spanish flu swept the country in 1919, Beatrix organized for a nurse to come and care for families in the village who had been struck down by the disease. The nurse would complete her rounds on a bicycle, and lived rent-free in a cottage that Beatrix owned near Hawkshead.

Girl Guides camped every summer on her farmland.

Gone but never forgotten

Towards the end of her life, Beatrix was too ill to get out of bed and see the countryside she loved so much. She died in 1943 at the age of 77. Her shepherd, Tom Storey, buried her ashes at Hill Top Farm. Only Tom knew where.

A Lasting Legacy

Beatrix gave all her land, which totalled more than 4,000 acres and fifteen farms, to the National Trust. It meant this countryside would be looked after for years to come.

The Lakes today

Today, people flock to the Lake District to enjoy its unspoilt beauty. It's possible to visit Hill Top Farm to see the house and its garden kept exactly as they were when Beatrix lived there.

Remembering Beatrix

Beatrix Potter was strong, creative and clever – a pioneering businesswoman and a fierce conservationist. The V&A Museum holds many of her letters, sketches, first editions and other items, keeping them safe for us all to enjoy.

Peter's success set Beatrix on a path that she never would have expected to venture down. Her long career as a writer gave her the financial independence to live the life she wanted at a time when women had very little say about what they could do.

Her books have sold over 250 million copies worldwide. And so the cheeky little rabbit that Beatrix drew more than a hundred years ago lives on.